Going Live in 3, 2, 1

Have You Got What It Takes to Be a TV Producer?

WITHDRAWN

by Lisa Thompson

Compass Point Books ⊕ Minneapolis, Minnesota

First American edition published in 2009 by
Compass Point Books
151 Good Counsel Drive
P.O. Box 669
Mankato, MN 56002-0669

Editor: Anthony Wacholtz
Designer: Ashlee Suker
Art Director: LuAnn Ascheman-Adams
Creative Director: Joe Ewest
Editorial Director: Nick Healy
Managing Editor: Catherine Neitge
Content Adviser: Chris Parrish, Senior Producer,
                    WOI-TV, West Des Moines, Iowa

Editor's note: To best explain careers to readers, the author has
created composite characters based on extensive interviews and research.

Library of Congress Cataloging-in-Publication Data
Thompson, Lisa.
  Going live in 3, 2, 1 : have you got what it takes to be a TV producer? / by Lisa
Thompson.
      p. cm.—(On the Job)
  Includes index.
  ISBN 978-0-7565-4082-1 (library binding)
1. Television—Production and direction—Vocational guidance—Juvenile
literature. I. Title.
  PN1992.75.S74 2009
  791.450232'023—dc22   2008038464

Image Credits: Greg Pease/Stone/Getty Images, cover (back); Tatiana Popova/
Shutterstock, 6; Dejan Ljamic/iStockphoto, 16; Dennis Sabo/Shutterstock,
18 (left); Yuri Arcurs/Shutterstock, 18 (right); AVAVA/Shutterstock, 21 (top);
Franck Camhi/Shutterstock, 21 (bottom); Pamela Moore/iStockphoto, 24; Krkr/
Shutterstock, 31 (top); Ron Sumners/iStockphoto, 35; Jan Tyler/iStockphoto,
37 (middle); Ton Haex/Shutterstock, 37 (bottom); Zsolt Nyulaszi/Shutterstock,
40; Catherine Yeulet/iStockphoto, 42 (bottom). All other images are from one of
the following royalty-free sources: Big Stock Photo, Dreamstime, Istock, Photo
Objects, Photos.com, and Shutterstock. Every effort has been made to contact
copyright holders of any material reproduced in this book. Any omission will be
rectified in subsequent printings if notice is given to the publishers.

Visit Compass Point Books on the Internet at *www.compasspointbooks.com*
or e-mail your request to *custserv@compasspointbooks.com*

Table of Contents

My Job

Monday

6 A.M.—Flight to Wildlife Wilderness Park for all-day location shoot for *Purple Lava*

Tuesday

9 A.M.—Meeting with my executive producer to go over budgets and possible pilot schedules for *Monster TV*

1 P.M.—Meeting with *Purple Lava* researchers concerning the list of guests for the show next week

Afternoon—Check final scripts for tomorrow's studio filming of *Purple Lava*

Wednesday

8 A.M.—Start studio filming for *Purple Lava*

Teens who will be auditioning for the host role on Monster TV

Thursday

10 A.M.—Casting for hosts of *Monster TV* with director

2 P.M.—Meet with graphics team about *Monster TV* titles and with the marketing team about promotional material

4 P.M.—Meeting with the writers of *Monster TV*

Friday

Check final edit for *Purple Lava* location footage to air Saturday morning

Go over production and shooting schedule for *Monster TV* pilot

TV Production

As a TV producer, I am the member of the production team who guides a project from beginning to end— that is, from the original idea of a television show to finding funding, budgets, scripting, filming, editing, and final distribution. It is a producer's role to make sure the project runs smoothly, comes in on budget, reaches its target audience, and is successfully completed.

Monday

It's not even 7 A.M. and already my cell phone has been running hot for the last half hour. We are scheduled to film segments on location at a wildlife park for my program, *Purple Lava*—a children's program with interviews, cartoons, and dares that is hosted by three teenagers. However, members of the camera crew have missed the flight because of heavy traffic around the airport. Luckily we were able to get them on the next flight. They'll now be late joining us on location, which affects our tight filming schedule. All filming must be done today because of budget and time constraints, so I am trying to juggle our filming schedule with the zoo staff.

As I sip my morning coffee on the bus to the wildlife park, I go over the scripts for the hosts. I am ready for whatever is in store. After years of working as a TV producer, I know things rarely, if ever, go as planned. When I was starting out in the industry, someone once told me, "The key to survival as a producer is always be prepared, remember everything can be negotiated, and laugh often." That was excellent advice!

PUN FUN

Recording 10 TV shows at the same time isn't even remotely possible.

TV Producers Work in Many Areas

Documentaries

Advertising

Game shows

Soap operas

News

Animation

Sports

Music television

Children's television

7

How I Became a TV Producer

I always wanted to work in television. At school I did well in English, and I originally thought about being a television reporter.

In college I did media studies as part of my bachelor's degree, and I majored in journalism. While in college I got work experience with a television production company. I also took on the role of producer/ writer/director for some student films in my last two years.

After college I got a job as a researcher at a production company that produced a science show called *Tomorrow's Technology*. Being a researcher for the show was a great learning opportunity. Right from the start, I was able to brainstorm and develop program ideas, assist writers in preparing scripts, brief and organize the on-screen hosts, and scout locations for stories.

Producing student films was a great experience.

Tomorrow's Technology,
Episode 6: Action!

There was also a lot of legal work involving copyright clearances, intellectual property and music, appearance fees, and issues relating to brought-in materials used for photo shoots.

Being a researcher was an invaluable start in the industry. I learned so much about negotiation, teamwork, crisis management, and getting a project finished, no matter what the obstacles.

After working on *Tomorrow's Technology*, I worked as a freelance producer for a production house before finally becoming the producer for *Purple Lava* and *Monster TV*.

Types of Producers

Staff producers are employed on a continuous basis for a production company or television station. They are often assigned to a specific project or department. However, in small television stations, a producer will often float between departments and projects.

The independent producer pitches ideas to studios.

Independent producers put together and sell production ideas to studios, distributors, network and cable television executives, and publishers. Independent producers are responsible for the bulk of all prime-time television programming. Independent producers are not employed on a continuous basis— they work on a specific project or on a freelance basis.

Executive producers are often less involved in the day-to-day production decisions than other producers. They delegate many production tasks to others and focus on developing new projects and concepts.

Producer hyphenates combine the role of writer, producer, and/or director. Writer-producer-directors immerse themselves in planning and the day-to-day production process. They have most of the control of the quality of the original idea to the final product.

PUN FUN Two weathermen each broke an arm and a leg in a car accident. They had to call in about the four casts.

Depending on the size of the project, there are also other kinds of producers who manage and are responsible for specific areas of a production.

Type of Producer	Responsibilities
Executive producer	supervising one or more producers and representing the TV studio
Co-executive producer	helping an executive producer with his or her duties
Supervising producer	supervising other producers; can take the place of the executive producer
Coordinating producer	managing two or more producers on a single project
Co-producer	working with other producers
Consulting producer	assisting writers with content, sometimes specializing in a certain area
Associate producer	handling tasks assigned by the executive producer; usually works through all three stages of the production
Segment producer	managing one segment of a program
Line producer	handling practical tasks, such as sound or editing, rather than creating original content

All types of producers need to work as a team.

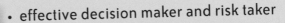

Qualities of a TV Producer

- effective decision maker and risk taker
- aptitude for solving problems
- ability to cope with changing situations and the pressures of tight deadlines
- ability to manage people and tasks
- creative and imaginative
- determined and self-confident
- excellent communication and organizational skills
- experience in techniques used in television production
- willingness to work on location and in unfavorable conditions with the possibility of long hours
- sense of humor

On-location shoots don't always go as planned.

Organization is very important.

Famous TV producers

Aaron Spelling (*1923–2006*)

Aaron Spelling was listed in the *Guinness Book of Records* as the world's most prolific producer. He began his career as an actor in Hollywood in 1953. He quickly decided he wanted to be behind the camera, working first as a writer and then as a producer. His first major hit came in 1963 with the show *Burke's Law*. During the 1980s, his show *Dynasty* was a major prime-time hit. In the 1990s, he produced *Beverly Hills 90210*, *Melrose Place,* and *7th Heaven.*

Mark Burnett (*1960– *)

Mark Burnett is a television producer known for his work with reality television. He produced the U.S. version of the series *Survivor* and *Eco-Challenge*. His company also set up such shows as *The Apprentice, The Restaurant, The Casino, Are You Smarter Than a Fifth Grader?,* and *Pirate Master.* Mark Burnett has won two Emmy awards.

David E. Kelley (*1956– *)

David E. Kelley is a multi-Emmy award winning writer and executive producer. He is also the creator of the television series *Picket Fences, Chicago Hope, The Practice, Ally McBeal, Boston Public,* and *Boston Legal.*

Stages of Production

Producers oversee a project through various stages of the production process. If the production runs over schedule or over budget in time or money, it is the producer who must step in and decide what to do.

The production process can be divided into three stages: preproduction, production, and postproduction.

Preproduction

This is the first stage of the production. During this stage, the producer works with the writers to prepare scripts for the episode. After brainstorming ideas for the episode, the producer and writers create a synopsis (summary or outline) of the idea. Then the writers do some research to make sure the information they include in the script is accurate. Next the producer and writers develop a storyboard—a layout of panels that show what should happen during the filming of the TV show. Once the storyboard is approved, the script is created.

During this stage, the producer has several other duties, including developing a production schedule, writing proposals for funding, hiring actors, creating a preliminary budget, and making sure that the plans for the show meet all the legal requirements. He or she must also secure any on-location sites that are needed for the show.

Screenplay

Manuscript

Production

Once all the plans are laid out in preproduction, the producer works with the director on the filming. At this stage, the equipment is set up and all props and settings are put into place. Rehearsals are typically done to spot any problems with the episode. After all the problems are worked out, filming begins.

Postproduction

After the filming of the show is completed, the producer works with the editor on the final touches at postproduction. This stage begins after the visual images and sounds have been recorded and includes editing, sound mixing, and special effects.

Colin is a pro at sound mixing.

Timeline of a TV Production

Program idea
An idea for an original TV show is developed

The draft script
After conducting some research and working through a few ideas, a draft script is created

Script analysis
The script draft is examined in order of scenes—known as the running order—to go over the segments, settings, and locations of shoots

Preliminary planning
The following issues are discussed:

- lighting, sound, and set design
- cost and special equipment
- postproduction techniques

Final script
After the planning for the show is completed and revisions to the draft script are made, the writers create a final script

Production meeting
The director notes shot-by-shot suggestions, problems, and changes; technical facilities and special effects are discussed

Specialist equipment
Sets are constructed, including planned lighting

Casting
Actors are cast for roles in the TV show

Rehearsals
The script is rehearsed both in and out of the studio setting

Camera script
The camera script includes details such as camera moves, positions, and cues

Technical run
This is a final prestudio rehearsal when problems are identified and solved; the studio is set up for lighting, stage design, sound equipment, and camera equipment

Camera rehearsals
Camera and sound crews follow the director's instructions

Taping
The program is recorded in sections or in its entirety

Off-line editing
The director and editor examine the recorded footage; the director decides on the order of the shots, potential editing points, and types of transitions

Online editing
Sequences are copied from the original tapes and sounds to make a show copy; any corrections in the picture—such as color, balance, or sound—are made, and titles, audio effects, background music, and special effects are added

Show copy
The final version of the tape is checked and given to the director and the producer for review

Transmission
The final tape is copied for distribution and archiving

Preproduction meeting for *Monster TV*

One of the programs my production company is trying to air is a music and lifestyle show for teenagers called *Monster TV*. We are still at the stage of securing funding to produce *Monster TV*, but we have enough money to produce a pilot of the show. A pilot is a sample episode of the show that is market tested before more episodes are aired.

Creating the set for the pilot episode

Monster TV is in the early concept stage when the idea is still being worked out and the goals, strategies, and look of the show are being defined. Today I am meeting with the executive producer of the program to talk about the progress of *Monster TV*.

PUN FUN

People who play musical instruments on TV have to stay tuned.

Meeting for *Monster TV*

Idea: *Monster TV* is a one-hour program of videos and interviews that revolves around the surf, gaming, skate, and music cultures. The format of the show has a collage-magazine feel with two studio hosts and a team of outdoor roving interviewers who are known in their fields of music, skating, surfing, or gaming.

Production goals and objectives for *Monster TV*

1. Create a new and fresh way of presenting teenage television that reflects current trends

2. Create informative and compelling viewing

Production goals and objectives

Getting funding is easier when a project's goals and objectives are clearly outlined. Members of the production team also need to be aware of them to avoid confusion and conflicts in the production process.

Audience Analysis and Research

An accurate estimate of the size and needs of your audience is essential for funding and marketing ideas. Producers also need to have an idea of the budget required to produce the show.

Demographics, groups of people with a common trait, are also very important to TV producers. Advertisers pay close attention to TV shows' demographics. Then they determine from which shows they want to buy time to advertise their products or services.

Advertising

Television advertisers design commercials to appeal to certain demographics. For example, during cartoons and children's television shows, there will be lots of ads for toys, fast food, and kids' movies. Advertisers want to know that their ads will be seen by the people most likely to buy their products.

PUN FUN

After ripping a page in his *TV Guide*, he was forced to tape his TV show.

Advertisers look at demographic group statistics such as:

- age
- race
- gender
- income
- education
- language
- religion
- special interests

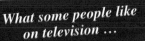

What some people like on television ...

... other people dislike.

Testing ideas

Commercial producers and distributors often rely on market research to estimate the size and the preferences of their audiences. The title of the project, who is involved, the subject matter, and a synopsis of the show may be given to test audiences. Their responses are then recorded and evaluated.

The Proposal

A proposal is a sales tool that describes the intended project and all aspects of the production. It should be professional and clearly written.

Proposal requirements:

- catchy opening statement
- outline of the purpose and objectives of the project
- your approach, structure, and style
- preliminary estimated budget
- shooting schedule
- equipment list
- summary of credits

Pitching a proposal can be nerve-racking.

Tiny props and sets

Sometimes television and movie producers use miniature models to shoot special effects. *Titanic* is one example of a movie that used models. Instead of shooting a life-sized ship in every scene, 45-foot (13.7-meter) models of the ship were used to make filming easier.

Monster TV Proposal

Producer: Celia Stewart
Director: James Wilks
Writers: Jason Holper and Eliza Easton

Monster TV will be a vibrant and fast-paced show that captures the adventure and passion of youth culture. It is a music and lifestyle show for kids 9 to 15 years old.

Each episode will consist of studio interviews, on-location stories, and music videos. The studio shooting schedule for the six episodes is two days. There are 12 on-location interviews that will be recorded over a period of six days. Research and preparation of the final scripts will be done within three weeks of the acceptance of the proposed treatment.

The budget will be approximately $80,000, depending on specific technical requirements of the script.

Getting Something on Paper

We meet with writers for *Monster TV*
Scriptwriters are key in the preproduction phase. Once the producer has outlined the main idea, the writers usually begin their own research, keeping in mind the producer's goals and objectives.

Scriptwriters usually determine the structure of a project by writing a detailed summary known as a treatment. It lays the groundwork for a script and is written in both the third person and present tense. Treatments are an important part to getting funding because they help everyone see the big picture. Before the treatment is prepared, a premise, synopsis, and several possible story outlines are drafted to help organize the show's theme and components.

Once a project receives funding and is given the green light to go ahead, the writer will then write a full script. The script provides a scene-by-scene description of settings, action, and dialogue or narration. It functions as a blueprint that guides the actual production.

This surf shot will look cool in the intro.

**Monster TV
Treatment**

The program will open with a montage of music, action, and audience shots. It then cuts to the music title track and more action scenes for the program.

Examples of action scenes include kids
- surfing
- skateboarding
- riding bikes
- playing in a park
- watching fireworks
- having bonfires
- mountain bike riding
- face painting
- playing jokes on each other

This series of shots is to give the look and feel of adventure and having fun. It has a golden tint to it and is a little scratched and drawn-over in postproduction to give it a moving diary feel.

Girls just wanna have fun!

We'll show some daring skateboarding tricks.

We need wild outdoor shots.

Scriptwriting basics

Scriptwriting for television shows can be divided into two basic categories:

- fiction (drama, soaps, miniseries, sitcoms)
- nonfiction (documentaries, news programs, live television, sports, talk shows, educational programs)

Scriptwriting formats

There are three basic script formats: full-page master scene, semi-scripted, and split-page.

Full-page master scene

This format is often used in single-camera, drama, and fiction-based programs. The script is organized into scenes that are numbered in consecutive order. All visual and audio instructions fill the page in one column.

Semi-script

This form is common for productions that cannot be scripted, such as sporting events. It is just a rough outline that allows for more freedom during the shoot.

Jason is one of our talented scriptwriters.

Split-page script

In this format, the visual information appears on one side of the page, and the audio on the other side. The wildlife shoot for *Purple Lava* is in a split-page script format.

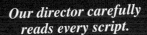

Our director carefully reads every script.

Video

Images of the penguins waddling around their enclosure. Shots of the penguins diving into the water and sliding down the water slide. Should be fast paced, flashing from one image to the next.

Close up shot of Kelly's face.

Medium shot of Ranger Robyn feeding a penguin a fish.

Medium shot of Kelly and Ranger Robyn.

Wide shot of Ranger Robyn leading Kelly through the enclosure.

Audio

High energy soundtrack and splashing noises. Include penguin noises over soundtrack.

KELLY (facing camera): "I'm here with Ranger Robyn, and she has the fantastic job of looking after the penguins at the wildlife park."

KELLY (directed toward Ranger Robyn): "Ranger Robyn, tell us about the special things needed to look after a penguin in captivity."

Ranger Robyn then discusses the penguins at the wildlife park.

Schedule and Budget Breakdown

I now have a rough script for the six pilot episodes of *Monster TV*. From this I can devise a shooting schedule and make sure each episode comes in under the budget. The shooting schedule indicates the total number of days of recording that will be required.

Title: **Monster TV**
Producer: Celia Stewart

Client: Kid TV Productions
Director: James Wilks

---

 1. Script (rights, research, writing, duplication) _____
 2. Staging (sets, costumes, location fees, props) _____
 3. Equipment (rental, lease, use fees)
 4. Special equipment (mounts, aerials, jet skis) _____
 5. Raw stock
 6. Duping (time code copies, off-line copies) _____
 7. Audio (effects, rights, fees, looping) _____
 8. Music (fees, rights, performances) _____
 9. Graphics (titles, animation, art) _____
10. Editing
11. Personnel (staffers, crew, guests) _____
12. Travel (transportation, accommodation) _____
13. Distribution (dubs, promotion) _____
14. Postage/insurance _____
15. Other _____
    _____

                              Subtotal   _____

| Overhead | _____ |
| Contingency | _____ |

                              Grand Total =   _____

Staying within the budget is a must.

Production management

When producers are managing a project, they need to break it down into parts so that it can be shot in the cheapest way possible. For example, if there are various scenes to be filmed on a ship, they will shoot all those scenes together on one day, even if it is out of order. This saves having to lease the ship for many days. Script breakdown sheets and budgets help producers manage the time and cost of the project.

I will have to book flights and reserve rooms at a motel for some of the on-location shoots.

While *Monster TV* is still in preproduction, my other program, *Purple Lava*, is in production. Today we will shoot the studio footage with hosts and guests for the episode that is to air this Saturday. Although it is only a 90-minute program, shooting takes a lot longer. It takes time to set up various camera angles, shoot each segment, wait for guests, and record promotional footage.

✔ Arrive at studio.

✔ Hosts go over their lines for the studio interviews.

✔ Meet the guests and give them a run-through of what's expected.

✔ Meet with director and studio floor manager to discuss problems, camera changes, and a timetable for the day.

✔ Keep everyone on schedule and on track during the day's shoot.

More than 60 years of air time

The longest running U.S. television network show is *Meet the Press*. The show started airing in 1947 and is still going!

A scary studio guest is coming in today!

Monster TV Update Meeting

We have now decided on our hosts. We are having one boy and one girl studio host, as well as a team of six rotating location hosts. Max and Lottie are the show's main studio hosts. Shooting of the pilot is to begin in three weeks. Camera and audio crews have been hired.

Max and Lottie begin learning their lines for the pilot episode.

The graphics team has made logos and promotional material for the show.

Theme music is prepared for the beginning of the show. A list of music we will use during the show is cleared for legal permissions and copyrights.

Peter helped design the logo for Monster TV.

Monster TV promotion shoot

Outdoor location shots with the two hosts have been created for promotion. Both hosts have individually inter-viewed a singer in the studio and a guest at a sporting event.

We scored an interview with a popular singer.

We want the Monster TV set to be fun and scary!

Max and Lottie are a match made in heaven!

Studio sets are designed and made. The director is putting together storyboards for the look of the show and how the studio footage is to be shot.

The director and I are pleased with how the hosts come across on camera. Both Max and Lottie look relaxed and like they are having fun, which is one of the key objectives for the program.

Postproduction

Editing

Editing is the craft of arranging, selecting, trimming, and combining sounds and visual effects after recording. Editing can take place during production or postproduction.

Visual editing terms

trimmed shots—unwanted portions can be removed from the beginning or the end of a shot

cut—direct, instant transition from one shot to the next

fade-out—first shot gradually disappears into black; when a new shot begins to appear, it is called a fade-in

dissolve—consists of an overlapping fade-out of the first shot and a fade-in of the second shot

transitions—ways of moving from one shot to the next

Sound mixing

Sound mixing is the process of blending sounds or sound tracks. This includes transition devices such as fades, cross-fades, and segues.

Studio microphone

There are three basic kinds of sound effects:

library effects—prerecorded on CDs and audiotapes

spot effects—specially recorded in the sound studio

actuality effects—recorded in the field

Looping

Automatic Dialogue Replacement, otherwise known as looping, allows speech sounds to be added and matched perfectly to prerecorded images. This means voice-overs and narration can be recorded and edited before the images are selected.

Special Effects

Today there are many kinds of production and post-production special effects that can alter prerecorded images and sound. They can also be created from scratch. They can be as high-end as completely reconstructed digital images or as basic as makeup. Producers need to have an understanding of the limits and scope of these effects so they know which to choose with the budget and time constraints in mind.

One of the advantages of creating special effects during postproduction is that it can save time and money. This is especially true if a scene needs to be reconstructed and actors and crew are called back to shoot some of the segments again.

Special effects are divided into seven basic categories:

1. *digital effects*—transitions, filters, compositing (grouping) of more than one image, morphing or changing images

2. *camera effects*—fast and slow motion and single-frame animation effects

3. *optical effects*—wipes and split screens

4. *models or miniatures*

5. *animation*

6. *physical effects*—wind, fog, smoke, rain, snow, fires, explosions, gunshots

7. *makeup*—makeup can transform an actor into anything from an alien to an animal

Chris, the director, wants to incorporate some split-screen visuals for the on-location footage in post-production. He also wants some freehand drawings over the footage to give it the feel of a diary. He has put together some examples with Jade, the editor, and I like what I see. As long as it doesn't affect the budget, I'll tell them to go for it.

Purple Lava Goes on Air

It's 7 A.M. on Saturday morning. I wake up, switch on my TV, and watch the *Purple Lava* wildlife special. The footage at the park looks excellent—not a hint of the trouble it was to shoot! The dusk footage with the animals at the end of the day looks great—just as we had planned it.

The episode of *Purple Lava* looks like a lot of fun without any evidence of the crazy rush behind the scenes to get it on air!

The sunset shots at the wildlife park look amazing.

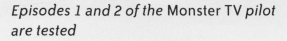

Episodes 1 and 2 of the Monster TV *pilot are tested*

Monster TV feedback

A sample tape of the first two episodes of *Monster TV* is sent out to our executive producer, a sample test audience of teens, and some television station executives who are interested in the show. They enjoyed the opening titles and think the pace of the show is good. They have a couple of suggestions for music artists and creative people to review, but they generally like the look and feel of the show. The response is positive for the most part, and it fires us up to finish off the other four episodes.

The sample audience enjoyed the pilot of Monster TV. *What a relief!*

Send Chat Attach Address Fonts Colors Save As Draft

To: CELIA STEWART

Cc:

Subject: Monster TV feedback

From: <Michael Anderson>

Dear Celia,

The interest from the sample audience was good! The station executives had a few overall comments. I'll send you more detailed comments in the coming days.

Overall comments
1. Keep the pace of the show strong with lots of scene changes in the music clips
2. There were great postproduction graphics.
3. There should be more interviews and profiles of young viewers.

Great work!

39

Selling a Project

Once a program is made, there are many markets into which it can be sold and viewed. It is vital that producers have a basic understanding of potential markets for a program.

There are many distribution and exhibition channels for programs, including broadcasting, cable, satellite, home video, multimedia, corporate, and in-house.

Producers need to be familiar with the technology used by distributors so they can tailor the production to the requirements. Producers also need to have an idea of the scope of profit for each market so they can promote the product accordingly. A production may not make it to commercial or cable broadcasting, but through marketing it can be very successful in the home DVD sales market.

PUN FUN The TV producer was going to prerecord a pie-eating contest, but he decided to do a live feed.

Shows that no longer air on television can also continue to make money on the home DVD market. Some television shows can also make money from CD releases, books, and merchandise.

Know the right people

Networking and having good working relationships is vital in this industry. Once you do land that important first job, you will need to maintain good working relationships with others involved in all parts of the production process.

Rating Success

Television rating figures mean life or death for a television show. They provide information about the show's popularity, which is essential for a show to remain on the air. They also give insight into the type of people who are interested in the show, which is important for producers when they are planning future content.

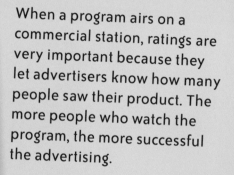

When a program airs on a commercial station, ratings are very important because they let advertisers know how many people saw their product. The more people who watch the program, the more successful the advertising.

Media research companies measure the number of people watching television shows and make this data available to advertisers and the media.

Nielsen Media Research gathers rating figures by choosing a small representative sample of viewers. They install a small, black box in their homes that tracks their TV viewing habits. The black box records when the TVs are on and what stations they are tuned in to. This information is then downloaded to the company's central computer every night. The research is worth billions of dollars, and programmers use this type of data to decide which shows to keep and which to cancel. Another way to measure TV ratings is the "diary" system, where viewers write down the shows they watch.

Super ratings

The Super Bowl draws an audience of more than 90 million people each year. As a result, advertisers love to get their products aired during the broadcast. Because of the game's popularity, it costs advertisers $2 million to $3 million for a 30-second commercial!

Follow These Steps to Become a Television Producer

Step 1

Finish high school with good grades, especially in English and media studies.

Step 2

Go to college to earn a degree in fields relating to TV production, such as broadcasting, media, communications, and journalism.

Step 3

Make your own documentaries or short films or be part of the production team for students who are studying filmmaking. You can also volunteer at television stations or production houses—it's a great way to make contacts in the industry and get your foot in the door.

Apply for an internship at a television station. Internships can be great opportunities to get real-life experience. Remember, most producers begin their careers in entry-level positions such as researchers or production assistants.

Step **5**

Join professional organizations or subscribe to publications from the media and film industry. Not only will this keep you up to date with news and events, it may also give you leads to job opportunities and the chance to make contacts.

Step **6**

Don't give up. In a highly competitive industry, you must make your own opportunities.

Opportunities for producers

Producers can work in a variety of jobs:

- full-time employee for a production company or a television station

- freelance or independent producer

- executive producer

- program writer

- technical editor

Find Out More

In the Know

- The longest-running daytime drama is *Guiding Light*. The soap opera has been on TV since 1960 and has aired more than 15,000 episodes.

- The longest-running game show is *The Price is Right*, which has been on the air for 35 years and has had more than 6,000 episodes.

- In 2007, there were more than 70,000 people employed as producers or directors in the entertainment industry in the United States. Of those, about 20,000 were in television or radio broadcasting, which makes up the second-highest field after the motion picture and video industry.

- As of May 2007, the U.S. Department of Labor estimates that the average hourly wage for a producer or director is $37.05, equaling $77,070 a year. The lowest 10 percent earned $28,980, and the highest 10 percent earned more than $96,670.

Further Reading

Dunkleberger, Amy. *So You Want to Be a Film or TV Director?* Berkeley Heights, N.J.: Enslow Publishers, 2008.

Parish, James Robert. *Jim Henson: Puppeteer and Filmmaker*. New York: Ferguson, 2006.

Reeves, Diane Lindsey. *TV Journalist*. New York: Ferguson, 2008.

Riedl, Sue. *Career Diary of an Animation Producer: Thirty Days Behind the Scenes With a Professional*. Washington, D.C.: Garth Gardner, 2003.

On the Web

For more information on this topic, use FactHound.

1. Go to *www.facthound.com*

2. Choose your grade level.

3. Begin your search.

The book's ID number is 9780756540821

FactHound will find the best sites for you.

Glossary

budget—estimate of costs for a project

copyright—law that gives ownership rights to the creator of a product and prohibits copying

cut—instant transition from one shot to the next

demographics—statistics about specific groups of people with common characteristics such as age, race, or religion

dissolve—transition consisting of a fade-out of a shot and a fade-in on the next shot

fade-in—transition where a shot gradually appears from a black screen

fade-out—transition where a shot gradually disappears into black

freelancer—someone who works for more than one employer and may not work on a regular basis

funding—money provided for a project

intellectual property—creative workers' rights that can be protected by copyright

internship—training program that provides on-the-job experience

networking—meeting and talking with people in your field

pilot—sample episode of a TV series

postproduction—stage when final touches are made to the filmed TV show

preproduction—stage when all of the preliminary work for the TV show is done

production—stage when the actual filming takes place

scriptwriter—person who creates the dialogue for a TV show

segue—transition from one segment to the next

storyboard—layout showing the story line of the planned TV episode

synopsis—summary or outline of a story

treatment—detailed summary of the story of a TV show

Index

Look for More Books in This Series: